What Love Would Say Coloring Book
By Connie Munde
© Copyright 2021

ALL RIGHTS RESERVED

With certain exceptions, no part of this book may be reproduced in any written, electronic, recording, or photocopying form without written permission of the publisher or author. The exceptions would be in the case of brief quotations embodied in critical articles or reviews and pages where permission is specifically granted in writing by the author or publisher and where authorship/source is acknowledged in the quoted materials.

Published by Shepherd Sanctuary Publishing
Coloring book: 978-1-7342828-4-9
What Would Love Say hardback: 978-1-7342828-0-1
What Would Love Say trade paper: 978-1-7342828-1-8
What Would Love Say eBook: 978-1-7342828-2-5
Library of Congress Control Number: 2019921149

Illustrators: Beverly Sealy, Kate Green, and Nada Hassanien
Book design: Rebecca Finkel, F + P Graphic Design, FPGD.com
Book Consultant: Judith Briles, The Book Shepherd

First Edition
Printed in USA

Because I am LIGHT

Slowed down enough to matter

so the hand of the Creator may touch me and I may touch back!

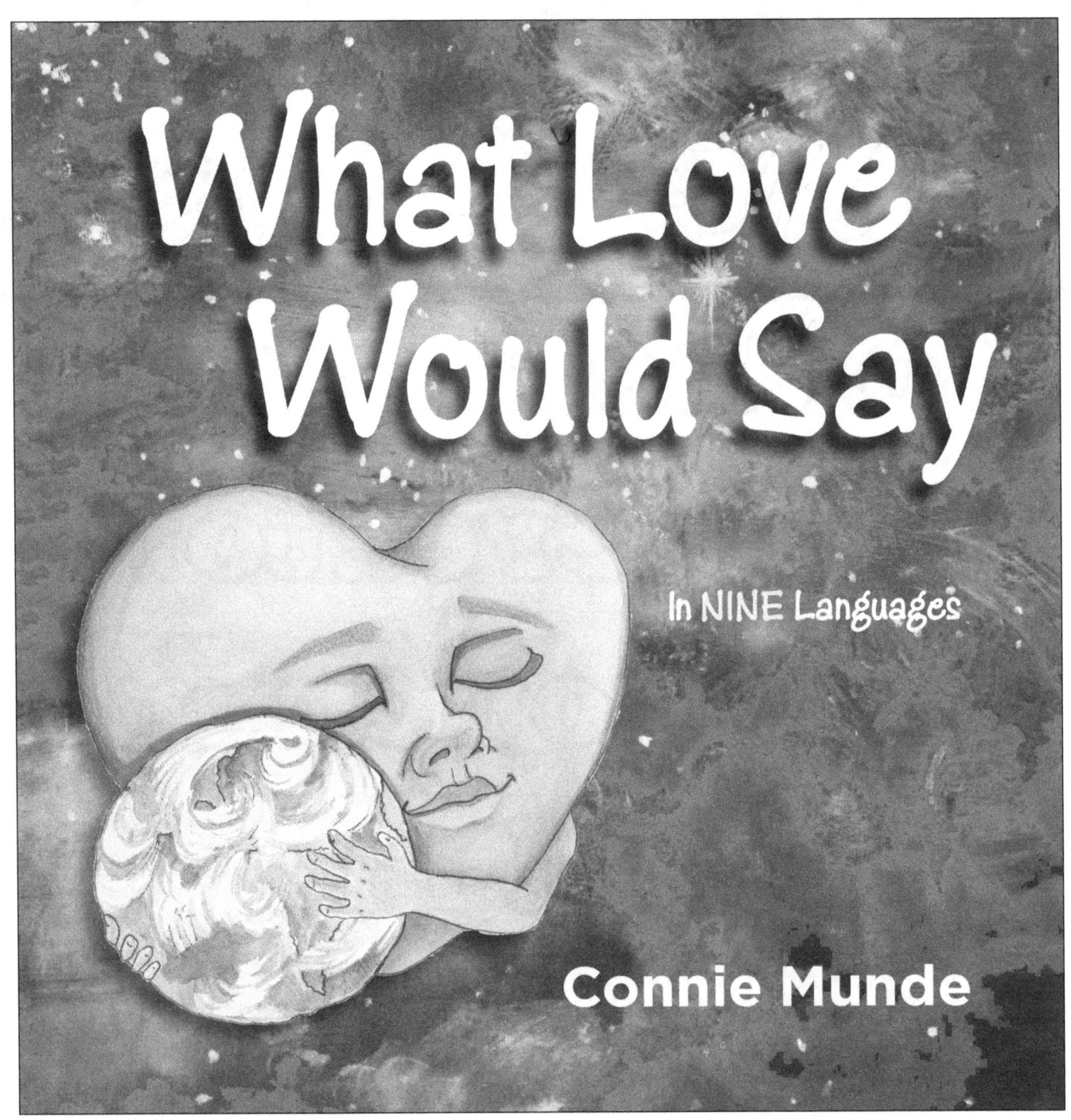

Check out the perfect companion book

for a deeper understanding of life.

www.ConnieMunde.com

is your resource for creating the best version of yourself!